INTRODUCTION

Of all the finch-like birds that are kept in captivity, there can be no doubt that the most popular one is the little Zebra Finch from Australia. These chirpy little birds have become so well known that they are now regarded as a domesticated species in virtually all countries where they are found. It is doubtful if any aviculturist has not kept at least one pair of Zebra Finches during his life, and many bird keepers were introduced to the hobby as a result of keeping these grassfinches.

The reasons why Zebras are so popular are numerous. They are very low priced; indeed, no other species can be obtained as cheaply. They are undemanding in their feeding habits, and they are extremely prolific breeders. They are available in numerous color varieties and they make excellent foster parents. Their virtues do not end here either, for they are also hardy birds and very sociable, so they can be included in mixed aviaries with no problems. In actual fact, they are

Zebra Finches are popular for many reasons, but especially because they're sociable, colorful and have an appealing song.

so friendly that this is not always appreciated by other birds trying to incubate eggs—Zebras will give them a hand given half the chance!

Of all the other finch-like birds, possibly only the Bengalese or Society Finch can rival the all-around qualities of Zebra Finches. As pet birds, Zebras are no less appealing for they are attractive without being unduly colorful, and they will happily breed in cages; their song is perhaps their only failing, it being a rather monotonous cheep cheep, but it is quiet and unobtrusive. They are extremely popular exhibition birds and have the advantage that a good show pair can be purchased at a very modest price compared with most other species.

HISTORICAL BACKGROUND

... same ... of ... or ... ut ... pose certain facts based on what was happening with other species. The Zebra Finch was first identified in 1817, and its Australian subspecies was first described in 1837. John Gould introduced the budgerigar to aviculture in 1840, and the first large shipment of budgies was possibly in 1861. It would be reasonable to assume Zebra Finches were also being received into Europe at this time. By 1879 Zebras were well known enough to be included in a book by C.W. Gedney, *Foreign Cage Birds*. By 1888, Zebras were certainly being bred consistently in European aviaries, so we may assume that the period of 1850-80 was the period that the Zebra Finch became a well-known aviary bird. In looking at a German advertisement dated 1889, it is interesting to compare the prices then asked for various species and ponder just how the times have changed.

It can be said that the little Zebra Finch, which was once quite an expensive foreign bird and highly regarded, has become the best value in the bird world!

In 1921 the first mutational color appeared in Australia, this being the white, and was followed in 1935 by the pied in Denmark. Whenever mutations appear in birds, they always increase the devotees of a species and as a result Zebras attracted many new bird keepers to their ranks. More mutations followed, and by the 1940s Zebras were very well established. In 1952 the Zebra Finch Society was formed in the UK, and this gave further impetus to the species' popularity. By 1958 Zebra Finches were so well established in aviaries that the Zebra Finch Society declared them a fully domesticated species. In 1960 Australia banned the export of any indigenous species of animal, and this gave added interest to the breeding of

A native of Australia, the Zebra Finch was introduced to Europe in the late 1800s and was a well-established cage bird by the turn of the century.

You'll find the dainty and dapper Zebra Finch at any bird show in the country, and his popularity is on the rise.

all Australian birds, including Zebra Finches.

The first all Zebra Finch bird show took place in 1974, and today the species is always very well represented at any bird show. 1972 was a special year for Zebras, for at the National Exhibition of Cage and Aviary Birds in the UK, a pair of white Zebras won the supreme award. Elsewhere in the world, the success story has been the same, and in Germany, Holland, Denmark, France, Japan, and the USA, these birds have become immensely popular. Of course they have always had a very strong following in their native country. Even in the previously designated Iron Curtain countries, the Zebra Finch is a very popular cage bird. There is no reason to believe their popularity will in any way diminish because new color mutations are always a possibility—as is the potential of introducing new colors as was done with canaries. When this happens, as it surely will one day, then even more people will swell the ranks of Zebra Finch supporters.

NOMENCLATURE

Any person who decides to pursue the hobby of bird keeping is strongly advised to have a basic understanding of the way in which all life forms are classified by scientists. Such a knowledge will be found to be most useful when checking data or searching for references on birds, as the system used to identify species is totally international in application, thus overcoming language barriers. Conversely, common names can create confusion and misunderstanding because often two or more names are used for the same species—and may be used for more than one species. As an example, the Zebra Finch is also known as the Chestnut-eared Finch and even as the Spotted-sided Finch, though neither of these two names have much following these days.

All birds belong to the class Aves, and this class is divided into a number of groups (known as ranks) such as the Psittaciformes (parrots), Anseriformes (ducks, swans, geese), and many other orders as they are termed. Zebra Finches belong to the order known as Passeriformes—the perching birds—which contains all of the songbirds and finches, the popular softbilled birds, the crows, and many more. The Passeriformes are divided into 60 families, each containing birds having numerous features in common with each other. Zebra Finches belong to the family called Estrildidae—the waxbills. There are many sorts of waxbills, so where a number are obviously very similar in all but minor details, they are placed within a rank called the *genus* (plural *genera*) so that each family is divided into many genera. Within each genus, there may be a number of clearly identifiable breeding populations, and if so, they are given the rank of species. By now

If you became an active bird hobbyist, you'll discover the Zebra Finch is also known as the Chestnut-eared Finch and the Spotted-sided Finch.

we have reached the individual birds. However, if it is believed that even within the same species there are clearly those types that are consistently different in some small detail, then they are given the rank of subspecies—they are the living examples of evolution in progress.

monotypic species—the only member of its genus. The Zebra Finch is placed in the genus *Poephila* by many experts but in the genus *Taeniopygia* by others, so you will see one or other of these in all reference books to this species, under the scientific name of *Poephila guttata* or *Taeniopygia*

Zebra Finches belong to the family Estrildidae, the waxbills, in which there are many other birds that differ only in minor detail.

A genus may contain just one species or it may contain many. For example, most ornithologists today consider that the very beautiful bird known as the Gouldian Finch cannot be placed, as in the past, in other genera and is distinct enough to be placed in its own—this being *Chloebia*; the Gouldian, *Chloebia gouldiae*, is thus known as a

guttata. The species name is always a binomial and is comprised of the generic name, which always commences with a capital letter, and the trivial or specific name, which always commences with a lowercase letter; only when the two are used *together* is a species identified.

If a subspecies is recognized, then the original type first

described has its trivial name repeated, thus forming a trinomial, and this subspecies is known as the nominate race. All other subspecies are given the species name plus their own epithet, which identifies them. In Zebra Finches the originally identified form did not come from Australia but from islands north of the continent and this is the nominate race *Poephila guttata guttata*, the later identified continental race being known as *Poephila guttata castanotis*. It is customary that the ranks up to and including the genus are always placed in a typeface differing from that of the text—thus italic is the usual choice, and in typewritten matter these ranks would be underlined.

AUTHOR NAMES

The first person to describe a species is known as the author, and it is usual that their names appear immediately after the species name. The date of the original description will then follow the author's name. However, the author may have placed the species in a different genus to the one that it is currently in—much having been found out about the species since it was first discovered. In such a case, the author's name is placed in parentheses. Additional information may be added below the species. This information indicates the article or book in which the original reference to the species description can be found. In the case of the Zebra Finch, the species classification.

Zebra Finch
Poephila guttata (Vieillot) 1817
Fringilla guttata Vieillot, *Nouv. Dictionnaire d'Hist. Nat.* 2nd ed vol XXI, p 233 (1817)
Anandina castanotis Gould, *Synop. Birds Australia*, 1, pl 10, 1837

From the above, it can be seen that Vieillot originally classified the Zebra Finch with the true finches of the family Fringillidae while Gould placed them with

These finches are classified as *Poephila bichenovii*, and are related to Zebra Finches by genus. Their common names are the Bicheno, Owl or Double-Barred Finch.

other weaver-finches (so-called because they weave nests in which to lay their eggs). As later ornithologists studied the various families of birds, some species were re-assigned to other genera, and even families, based on the believed relationships of one species to another.

   The genus *Taeniopygia* was used to house the Zebra Finches, which were considered a monotypic species for a period of time, but current thinking is that they are closely related to the other members of the genus *Poephila* which are:

   P. bichenovii Bicheno, Owl or Double-barred Finch

   P. personata Masked Finch

   P. acuticauda Long-tailed Grassfinch or Heck's Grassfinch

   P. cinta Black-throated, Parson or Diggler's Finch

NATURAL HISTORY

In the wild state, the nominate race of the Zebra Finch, *Poephila guttata guttata* is found on the Lesser Sunda islands of Sumba, Flores, Timor and other smaller Islands of the chain. The Australian subspecies, *P.g. castanotis*, is found throughout much of the continent, especially in the dry interior. It is absent from the wet rain forests of the coastal areas.

Zebras are very social birds and are found in flocks that will number from 25-100 pairs; during very dry periods considerable numbers may share a water hole. The availability of surface water is a crucial factor in their whole pattern of life, for while it is believed they can go for very prolonged periods without water, nonetheless they stay as close to it as possible. However, among the finches of the world, there is little doubt that the Zebra has adapted very well to arid conditions. It is able to drink water containing a much higher level of salt than most other species. Likewise, Zebra Finches are able to retain water that most other birds would release via their urine, this again enables the species to endure long periods without drinking.

Zebras, along with Gouldian, Star, Bicheno, and other finches that survive in desert-like conditions, drink by immersing their beaks into the water and sucking it up—after the fashion of pigeons. This enables them to drink faster (thus quickly leaving water holes, where they are in danger of attack by predators) and also to suck water from droplets on vegetation, rocks, and other places that would not be as easy if conventional bird drinking methods were used. Zebras drink during the middle of the day, whereas many other species will drink at first light or during the early parts of the day.

BREEDING

The Zebra Finch is probably one of the fastest-breeding birds in the world, and this again is an adaptation to the severe climatic conditions in which it lives. In the arid interior of Australia, rain is not at all seasonal as it is in coastal areas. It is quite unpredictable in when it will appear. As a result, Zebras are rain-induced in their breeding cycle and will immediately commence nest building at the onset of rain. This cycle is such that the species will double or triple brood in a year—or they may not breed at all if the rains do not appear. The pair bond is strong, and it is believed that it is for the life of the pair until one dies at which time the other will then take on a new mate.

In the less severe areas of Australia, breeding is more regular and will usually be throughout the year with the exception of the coldest winter

In nature, Zebra Finches live in flocks of 25 to 100 pairs and commonly share a watering hole, from which they drink in the middle of the day.

months, which are June and July. In spray-irrigated areas, the species also breed throughout the year with the exception of July.

Courtship

Unlike most other grassfinches and other finches, Zebra cocks do not parade with a stalk of grass. Courtship begins with much beak rubbing followed by the male approaching the female in a series of little hops, during which he will display his tail feathers and sing continually. He will also raise his cheek and abdomen feathers. If receptive, the hen will quiver her tail and mating will take place.

NestBuilding

The rains will bring forth the seeding grasses on which Zebras feed, and also many insects, so Zebras waste no time in preparing their nest. The cock will usually suggest sites to the hen, and after deliberation she will accept one of them. It has been noticed that where water is more reliable throughout the year, the hen alone builds the nest with the cock acting as the transporter of materials. However, in the interior of the continent, both birds will build, this no doubt being because of the need to speed up the whole breeding cycle. The nesting sites vary considerably—as does the quality of the building. Thick bushes are preferred but Zebras will build in any suitable place including on the ground in grass, in the old nests of other birds, tree hollows, termite mounds, posts, and even in the large twiggy nests of birds of prey—this is a very adaptable species!

The outer nest is made of twig or roots that get softer and smaller as they near the actual breeding pan, which is covered with feathers, soft grass, rabbit fur, and any other material the pair is able to acquire. The nest may contain a dome, but it may also be an open affair and is certainly not the beautiful structure made by the true weaver species.

Zebra Finches line their nests with soft materials they scavenge from their environment, like grasses, feathers or rabbit fur.

Eggs

The number of eggs laid will be four or five on average but can vary from two to eight. They are pure white, and the size is also variable, even within the same clutch, but $5/8$" (15mm) is about the mean average.

Incubation

Both birds incubate the eggs, each taking turns of about one and a half hours. Each will leave the nest on hearing the call note of the approaching mate so that they do not change over in the nest itself. During the night, both birds will remain in the nest. Incubation will usually commence after the fourth egg has been laid (and they are laid one each on successive days) and will last from 12-16 days depending on the temperature.

Fledging

The young chicks grow very rapidly, and, depending on how attentive the parents are at feeding them, they will usually leave the nest by the age of three weeks. They return continually to spend the night with their parents, who will continue to feed them, on a reducing basis, until they are about another ten days older, at which time they are fully independent. At that time they may leave the nest to search for their own roosting nest or they may stay in their nest if the female decides she would like a new nest for her next round of eggs.

The Molt

Young Zebra Finches commence their molt when they are about 8-9 weeks old. It is concluded over a 4-7 week period, so that a youngster is itself capable of breeding in the wild from about the age of three months. This is amazingly fast, and I cannot bring to mind any species that matures quite so quickly.

their nests from other species—even those that may be somewhat larger than themselves. They are wary birds and do not let humans approach them as closely as certain other species might. They have adapted, however, to urban life and can be found around most human settlements, where they take full advantage of the introduced crops and the availability of water.

Zebra Finches are quick breeders and both parents incubate the eggs, which hatch in two to three weeks depending on the temperature.

SOCIABILITY

In the wild, Zebras Fiches are extremely sociable and clearly are aware of those that make up their community. They will visit each other's nests without problem—but will not tolerate Zebras from another community. They are very tough little birds in defending

FEEDING

Seeding grasses form the basis of the Zebra Finch diet. They are collected from the ground, or the bird will flutter up to peck off half ripened seeds—they are not known to cling to the grasses as do many other species. They will consume both native and sunlight from which the birds cannot escape. They should be as close to your eye level as possible not only for ease of watching the birds but also because if you are looking down on birds it intimidates and thus stresses them, increasing the risk of illness.

If you have a number of birds, then maybe a birdroom can be made available, or you may house the cages in a garden shed or similar structure. If used in tiers, then always allow space between each tier for air to circulate. Do not attempt to keep too many cages in a small area. You need to allow for a working surface as well as for seed storage bins, equipment, and other needed items. If you plan to become a breeder, then it will pay you to visit a number of birdrooms of established aviculturists in order to pick up design ideas. You are certainly advised to subscribe to a national avicultural magazine. Membership in your local or national Zebra Finch or foreign bird club is also very worthwhile.

PENS

A pen is really only a very large cage. It can be part of a room containing cages as well, or the entire available space can be sectioned into large pens. A pen can be incorporated into your living room to great effect, and I have seen many superb units built into alcoves and made to be an integral part of the living area. These pens can contain just Zebra Finches or a number of finches of different species. The wire to use for pens is welded wire of about 19G (Gauge) with hole dimensions of 2.5 x 1.25

cm (1 x .5 in). With a pen you are able to be more creative and add large branches of natural woods as well as maybe a few potted plants to give effect—the advantage with most finches is that they are not destructive to plants as are the parrot-like birds.

For those who have limited aviary space, then a number of large pens in a birdroom would be of greater benefit than having all the space taken up by cages. It is always better to keep fewer but fitter birds than to have many, with little or no good flying space.

AVIARIES

The potential number of aviary designs is unlimited—or rather, limited only by the size of your cash flow! Aviaries can be purchased ready-made for self-assembly, or they can be designed and totally built by the bird keeper. Whichever option is taken, there are certain basic criteria that need to be incorporated in any aviary.

Site

Choose a position that is sheltered, maybe by a wall or trees, yet is not directly under these. In the case of trees, the ground will be very wet in winter months, the falling autumn leaves will be a continual problem, and the droppings of perching wild birds will greatly increase the risk of introducing illness into your aviary. Further, depending on the species of tree, toxic substances may be released by the branches periodically and, finally, birds of prey and cats can frighten the birds if they are perched or sitting above the aviary. In the case of walls, they provide similar vantage points for predators and also enable mice and rats to jump onto the roof netting. It is always better if the aviary stands on the highest ground in your garden as this facilitates quicker drainage of rain. Conversely, if at a low point, then the aviary will always be on damp ground during inclement weather.

The aviary should face south or droppings, and those of the aviary birds, with the result that the disease risk increases the longer the aviary is in place. Years ago, many aviaries were built in such a way that they could be moved to a different spot on a rotational basis in order that the earth could lay fallow for a year or so, but this is rarely seen these days.

Concrete can be covered with gravel to improve the esthetic appeal, and various shrubs can

This lush aviary has everything a captive Finch could want: plenty of space, sunshine, shady areas, and a natural habitat.

east in the northern hemisphere and north or east in the southern hemisphere as such aviaries will benefit most from the sunshine while being protected by their shelters from the worst of the winds and rains.

Base

The most hygienic base is concrete or paving slabs, as bare earth accumulates wild bird be planted in pots; small bushes can be planted into the earth in small spaces left for them between adjoining slabs. The entire perimeter of the aviary should be slabbed to form a pathway. Incorporate a water channel to take away rain.

Aviary Flight

It is recommended that the flight be made up of separate

Zebra Finches love to take baths, though a stone or ceramic container is better than plastic, which can be slippery.

provision of a concrete bath either at floor level or on a pedestal will be much appreciated. It should be shallow and contain one or two stepping stones into it—plastic is slippery so it is not recommended.

Exterior Lights

There are two reasons why lights are beneficial at night. The first is to reduce injury to the birds as a result of night frights. Many birds are killed each year because they have been startled into flight at night and crash into the aviary wire or fall to the floor and do not move because they cannot see. The light need not be overbright but should be sufficient to give some illumination. The other benefit is that it deters potential bird thieves who unfortunately seem to be on the increase in these turbulent times we live in.

A low wattage night-light in the shelter will also be beneficial. This can be a blue bulb—any startled birds can thus easily return to their perches.

Security Alarms

There are numerous systems on the market in varying prices, and they are worth considering. Even closed-circuit TVs are becoming of interest to bird keepers. It is not always the value of the birds in purely financial terms that is important but the years that may

flight, imitating the natural situation in bushes and trees.

Antipredator Netting

Loose plastic netting or large-hole chicken wire can be placed about one inch above the roof of the flight. This will distract at least most birds of prey from alighting on the roof and thus frightening your birds. Nor do cats like to walk on surfaces that "give" and are full of holes.

Closeable Pop Holes

It is useful if the entrance hole from the shelter to the flight can be opened and closed from either the shelter end or from outside of the flight. This is easily arranged by having a sliding door that is held up by wire that goes around a simple pulley and then to the aviary exterior.

Bath

Zebras enjoy bathing, and the

have gone into building a strain of birds that may justify extra security of aviaries and birdrooms.

Ionisers

The dust that does not easily settle in a birdroom, together with airborne microbes, carries disease risks that can be neutralized to a large degree by the use of an ionizer. These devices are now very popular and inexpensive to purchase and run—they simply fit into a light holder. The negative ions they release engulf particles in the air and make them heavier; thus they fall to the floor and are simply swept up with normal debris. To be effective, they really need to be in continual operation, but their running costs per year are very small indeed, so they are certainly recommended.

Dimmers

There are many light dimmers now produced for birdrooms. They automatically reduce the light intensity to a low level and increase it as required; this enables you to maintain twelve-hour light cycles, which are useful with tropical species.

Infra-red Lamps

I consider these lamps absolutely essential to a bird breeder—even a pet owner. A sick Zebra can be dead before you hardly have time to ponder what to do about it. Simply supplying heat can work miracles—such is the pace of the metabolism in birds, which out of necessity are unable to carry much reserves of fat or anything else. Infra-red lamps can simply be attached to a breeder cage and will maintain the required temperatures that would

This round cage is attractive for viewing your finches, who will want to perch on the swing hanging from the top.

otherwise be difficult for you to provide. They can be used effectively when rearing chicks so they are a good investment at a low price.

Incubators

These are not as important to Zebra breeders as they are to breeders of other species but are mentioned for completeness.

QUALITY OF BIRDS

Birds required as pets can be purchased from most pet shops. In some cases, the birds may be closed-ringed. These rings are placed on the birds when they are only a week old and serve as permanent identification tags. They will be stamped with a year date and a code number and are the *only* way you can verify the age of the birds you buy. Rung birds are important to pet owners if they wish to be sure of getting young birds or birds of reasonable quality.

As Zebras are not expensive ultimately creating your own carefully bred line.

It will certainly pay dividends for you to visit a number of bird shows where you can see the various colors, meet Zebra Finch breeders, and generally get to know whose birds are considered to be of good type (given that all breeders will tell you theirs are!).

When choosing your birds, look them all over for signs of good health and bad.

birds you are advised to purchase the finest pairs you can—not necessarily current winning birds, but those from successful stock, so you know you are building on good foundations. This will save much time in the long run. If the breeder has developed a strain over many years, then you should purchase two or three pairs. These birds should not be mixed with others purchased elsewhere, as you will want to develop your own strain carefully. Maybe two additional pairs purchased from other good stock will give you two separate lines to work with,

HEALTH

A good breeder will not sell you unhealthy stock—nor indeed will a reputable pet shop, as they will want your repeat business on equipment, seed, and other items. However, sadly, there are those who are less than honest, but if you have looked around beforehand it is unlikely you could be sold unhealthy birds.

First of all, stand back a while and study the birds to see if they are hopping about from perch to perch, and not just because you have startled them into action. Their eyes will be round and clear

This fellow is a fine specimen with round, clear eyes, no broken feathers and tight feathering.

and their beaks correctly aligned. There will be no signs of discharge from either eyes or nostrils. The legs will be clean and with no sores on the feet or missing toes, nor any signs of deformity. The feathers will be very tight and laying close to the body. The odd broken feather is no problem, as it will be replaced at the next molt; but feathers missing to the degree that they have created a bald spot is another matter and should be avoided. Birds with bald spots are probably feather pluckers, and this is a very difficult habit to cure once a bird starts doing it. Of course, plucked feathers from the head must have been the work of another bird, so this is a different matter. Even so, I would avoid such birds, as there is no need at all to commence with other than superbly fit and good looking stock.

When birds sleep, they do so perched on one leg, and then they turn their heads 90° and tuck them into their lower necks; they then fluff out their feathers, and the air between them warms up to keep them snug and warm. When a bird is ill, it will perch on both feet, feathers fluffed up and head drooping forward. Just occasionally, a bird may sleep with its head forward and both feet perched yet it may not be ill. The condition of the eyes will give you a good idea and experience will teach you how to tell the difference.

QUARANTINE

Once you have purchased your birds and transported them home, they should go through a three-week period of quarantine to see that they are well and not incubating any illness. They should initially be given seed and water and then be left in peace to settle down. You should always check on what they have been fed so you can continue in the same manner until the birds are fully acclimatized to their new home. Once you are satisfied the birds are fine, then they can be introduced to their new quarters. If this is an aviary, let them into it during mid-morning when the air is warmer. That will give them the rest of the day to explore and find suitable roosting sites—and to find out where their food is.

If the birds have never been in an aviary, or indeed exposed to the colder air outside, do not release them into flights during the winter—indoor pens are the better place until the spring comes around.

A head-on, close-up view of two females and two males—all alert and healthy looking.

The band on this male's leg is stamped with his birth date. These bands are the only means of verifying a Zebra Finch's age.

WHEN TO BUY AND BREED

This is not a crucial point with pet birds, as they will be living in a protected environment. If birds are to be released into display or breeding aviaries, then I would purchase in the spring, as this gives them the whole of the summer in which to become fully acclimatized and ready for the colder autumn and winter. I would not be unduly concerned whether new purchases breed in their first year, though this is likely with Zebras.

COMPATIBILITY

If a newly acquired pair is to be introduced to a colony of Zebras Finches, or into a mixed finch collection, this must be done with careful observation to see that the acquired birds are neither bullied, nor bully others. It must be

FEEDING

Zebra Finches are possibly the easiest of all birds to feed and can survive, and apparently do quite well, if only one type of seed is fed to them—such as yellow millet or panicum millet. However, such a Spartan diet is certainly not recommended as it will be deficient in a number of essential constituents that will be needed if the birds are expected to remain in good health, and especially if they are to be used for breeding.

It is always sound husbandry to have one's stock willing to eat from a variety of foods because we can not always be sure of the availability of each seed type—nor of its price. However, food preferences are acquired at an early age and unless a bird is accustomed to variety then it can be very difficult to pursuade it at a later date to change from one seed to the other. For this reason feed a variety of foods from the nest onwards so chicks do not become finicky adults. Obviously, all birds will show preference for a given seed even if they accept a range and so a careful watch should be made at feeding times so you can determine what is the favored choice.

FOOD VALUE

All food items do not have the same value to a bird and each fits into a basic type, depending on its constituents. Some are needed to provide muscular activity and these are known as carbohydrates as they are rich in sugars and starch (both of which are relatively simple compounds that can quickly be oxidized in the body to release energy). Examples are most seeds or grains and their products—bread, biscuit, oatmeal, bran and similar. A bird cannot afford to carry excess weight which would reduce its flying speed, so its metabolism is rapid and this means birds need to feed often but in small amounts. Finches, especially Zebras, thus need a good percentage of carbohydrate seed in their basic diet. Panicum millet, yellow millet, white millet and canary seed are the favored choice—with the first two named accounting for about 80% of the total seed consumed (this will vary from bird to bird). Yellow millet is often given in the form of millet sprays and this can be fed as it is or it can be soaked for 24 hours in fresh water, shaken, and then fed. It is much appreciated in both forms.

In order to replace worn muscles and to repair damaged bodily parts a bird needs protein—this, of course, being essential for youngsters as it also provides new tissues as the bird grows. Protein is found in seeds and in all animal products so these should both be provided. In actual fact, protein seeds are deficient in certain essential amino-acids (of which proteins are made) so animal protein is especially valuable for breeding birds with chicks to rear. Examples of protein rich seeds are linseed (21%), rape (20%), hemp (18%), and niger (17%). It happens that seeds rich in protein are also low in carbohydrate, for white and yellow millet each have about 66% of this latter compound.

Birds obtain insulation from cold, as well as energy reserves, from fats, and protein seeds are also rich in fats, especially maw and rape which have about 40% by content. These seeds are also rich in minerals (about 6%) while niger is the richest in this latter compound (7%). If a bird is short of carbohydrate then it will convert stored fats into energy and once these are used up it will convert body tissues, i.e., muscle, into energy; when this happens the birds breastbone will start to show and the condition is known as "going light." Your birds should never get into such a state.

It will be appreciated that a pet bird, or one caged, will use up less energy than an aviary bird so the amount of protein-fat seeds must be carefully rationed least your birds suffer from the

A pair of Zebra Finches enjoying one of their favorite treats, millet spray. With their rapid metabolisms, these birds need to eat often.

opposite problem of becoming overweight. The best times for these are during the winter and during the breeding period when they will be appreciated by the parents. Animal protein can be given in the form of bread and milk or via one of the prepared softfoods produced for canaries. Some breeders add honey to these softfoods but this carries the risk of attracting wasps so care should be exercised. Cheese and egg yolks can be added to mashs, indeed any animal protein suitably mashed can be given according to individual tastes.

GREENFOOD

All birds enjoy greenfood to a greater or lesser degree and Zebra Finches are especially fond of chickweed, celery, dandelion and, of course, any seeding grasses. But any greenfoods can be tried on your birds though be sure, in all cases, that it is washed, otherwise harmful chemicals from spraying could result in digestive disorders. It is better to attach greenfoods that are on stalks to the aviary wire in bunches and this is because if they are breeding Zebras will often take such stalks or grasses

Your local pet shop will supply products that will enable you to grow and offer your bird fresh home grown greens. Photo courtesy of Four Paws.

Greenfoods like the lettuce leaf these Zebra Finches are nibbling at are rich in vitamins and should be a regular part of the diet.

and deposit them in their nest thus creating sandwich situations with the eggs—not the most desirable state for the eggs at the bottom!

Greenfoods are rich in vitamins which are essential for balanced metabolic processes. Fruits also are rich in vitamins so always offer these. Oranges, apples and berries should be suitably cut into small pieces to form a salad which can be placed in a pot dish. Any perishable foods must be removed each day—not that the birds are likely to eat soured food but it is a potential health hazzard to them by virtue of the bacteria it attracts.

MINERALS AND GRIT

Birds need a whole range of what are called trace elements, examples of which are iron, copper, iodine, sulfur, mangenese, cobalt and many more. These are found in seeds, greenfood and most other foods, so supplementary addition should not be required under normal conditions. Grit, however, is vital to seedeating birds as it helps crush the seed in the gizzard into a pasty constituency that is then absorbed into the body. As the grit looses its sharp edges so it is expelled by the bird in the feces and needs to be continually replaced. It is available in the correct size from your pet shop and can either be scattered on the cage floor or fed in small pots.

Another essential mineral is calcium, which is needed for the formation of bone and for healthy eggshells. It can be supplied in the form of cuttlefish bone which is clipped to the cage or aviary wire, or it can be crushed into a powder and sprinkled on the seed-or softfood when the latter is given. A breeding hen's calcium intake rises dramatically so ensure there is always ample available to her otherwise she and the eggs will have problems. Crushed oyster shell or crushed eggshells can also be supplied as they are rich in calcium.

WATER

It was mentioned earlier that Zebras are believed to be capable of going without water for quite long periods—however, this fact has not been proven in the wild state but by experimental situations, and certainly your birds should *always* have water available to them. Naturalists state that wild Zebras drink daily and are indeed used as indicators of where water is by aboriginal peoples and travellers of Australia's inhospitable interior. In their excellent book on the Gouldian Finch, Evans and Fidler (1986) feature a table of the water budget of the Zebra Finch which, after allowance for water gained from food and seed, and water lost from feces and bodiy evaporation, results in a daily deficit of 0.97 g. This must be

This feeder is convenient for an aviary housing many birds, but is too large for the average cage.

replaced daily unless the bird is to commence drawing it from bodily tissue—which will ultimately upset other processes.

FEEDING SUPPLEMENTS

I have read articles that will state birds had stopped or reduced their breeding ability until fed with a given vitamin supplement. I may of course be totally wrong, but when birds need to be given concentrated proteins or vitamins then something is going wrong somewhere.

From what scientists tell us, the balance of vitamins and minerals in bodily tissues needs to be very precise in certain instances—an excess can be as damaging as a deficiency, for one vitamin can undo totally what another does. This said, if your birds seem lacking in some way then the wisest course of action is to

A variety of healthy seeds and grasses clipped to the side of the bird's cage supplies some of the energy-rich food active Zebra Finches require.

These small buds are canary seed, another excellent source of carbohydrate for the Zebra Finch.

consult a veterinarian who is known to specialize to some degree in birds. If there is a vitamin imbalance then he will prescribe the correct remedy. The problem may be a simple nutritional omission, it may be hereditary resulting from inbred stock becoming infertile, or it may simply be through lack of exercise. The possibilities are numerous and I cannot believe that simply adding this or that should be a wise path to follow without careful advice on the subject. Put your faith in a good wholesome and complete diet rather than reliance on concentrates. Maybe a chat with a good "old fashioned" breeder will reap handsome profit—they continue to breed superb birds by well-proven methods.

This Zebra Finch enjoys a well-rounded diet: seeds for carbohydrates and fat, and fruits and vegetables for vitamins and sugar. She also needs grit and protein.

PRACTICAL BREEDING

There are two ways in which Zebra Finches can be bred: either controlled or uncontrolled. The controlled is when they are paired according to color and bred in their own cage, pen, or aviary. The second method is when they are bred in aviaries or pens in work once the birds are in the aviary and able to have second thoughts about the choice *you* made!

BREEDING CONDITION

No birds should be paired up unless they are both in fit

Zebra Finches will choose their own mates, or you can choose them for them. Whichever way you go, make sure both birds are fit.

which two or more pairs are allowed to select their own mates. It is possible to influence uncontrolled breeding in some cases simply by introducing pairs to each other in cages. Once a bond has *apparently* been created, release them into an aviary. I have to say *apparently* because this does not always condition. The rearing of the young, rather than the laying of the eggs, is what really drains a hen of energy and, of course, the cock, as both birds share this duty in Zebra Finches. Before the breeding season commences, ensure that the birds are given ample time in an aviary to work off any fat they may have added over winter and during the show season. Exhibition birds may carry a little more weight than breeding birds. Prior to the planned breeding season, you should give the pairs a little extra protein seed and some softfood so that, in the hen's case, she has the extra nutrients to pass to the yet unborn chicks. The cock will also benefit from this, and it gets them accustomed to it so that when the eggs hatch they will readily take it to feed to the chicks.

The best time to breed is in the spring, when you have the increasing hours of daylight and the air temperature is getting warmer. However, Zebras will breed throughout the year if permitted, and many bird keepers breed in the winter in their birdrooms. The cocks and hens are best separated when not being bred; otherwise you will find eggs being laid haphazardly all through the year. The fact that no nest boxes are available will not stop these little finches from finding some suitable receptacle!

You should not expect all of your pairs to go to nest at the same time. Zebras can be very unpredictable in spite of their well-deserved reputation for being prolific. Indeed, there are occasions when some pairs will not breed at all, and for no apparent reason, when in previous years they have been very reliable.

SELECTING PAIRS

The object of any sound breeding program should not be to produce the occasional brilliant bird but to consistently raise the overall standard of your stock. This can only be achieved by careful selection of prospective pairs, applying genetic knowledge, rigid selection of stock retained, and by sound husbandry in respect to feeding and accommodations. This is not easy to do, as often you will have to compromise along the path to your objective.

When selecting pairs, you will be looking for birds that are as similar to each other as possible in their size, overall markings, and color—including their beaks. If a bird has a small failing, let us say it is on the small side, then select a mate which is of an ideal size. Never pick one that is slightly oversized as this sort of compensatory mating actually increases the genetic variability of your stock, which is not the objective.

You will have given considerable thought to your following season's pairings well before breeding is put in hand, You will have made decisions by consulting your record cards, which have been kept over the years and thus give you a full background history to your stud to that point in time. However, initially, you will not have the benefit of such cards, which is why it is essential that you buy your breeding stock from a reputable source. In this way you will at least know the genetic state of the birds and, having seen much stock of the supplier, will be able to check its overall quality.

Zebra Finches aren't too particular about their nests, and they'll make any nook or enclosure—even this coconut shell—a happy home for their young.

NEST BOXES

Having satisfied yourself that your pairs are in good breeding condition and having selected the pairs to be used, the next thing is to introduce them to their breeding cage, pen, or aviary. If they are compatible and do not start fighting with each other continually, then the nest box can be introduced. The pair will, after a few days, start to build their nest.

The most popular style of nest box for Zebras is a simple cube of about 13 cm (5 in), which contains an entrance hole and a perch just below this. It should have a hinged lid so that you can inspect the nest periodically to see if all is well. These nest boxes can be purchased from pet shops or made from plywood. Some breeders prefer to use nest boxes in which half of the front is cut away so that the nest is easily seen, while others will use wicker receptacles with a domed hood. Zebras are very accommodating where nest boxes are concerned and have been known to use plant pots, budgerigar nest boxes, feeding dishes, indeed anything that will hold the eggs.

If you plan to breed your Zebras in cages, it is better if the nest box is fitted to the outside, so that it can be inspected while creating the least disturbance to the parents. It also affords more room

You can see how the finches lined this basket-style nest with grasses to cushion the eggs.

The male Zebra Finch looks in on the eggs during a moment when the hen is away. He is ready to do his time in the nest.

in the cage. In aviaries, it is best sited in the shelter or in a covered part of the aviary. Where numerous pairs are being bred on a colony system, at least two nest boxes per pair should be sited, and in similar positions. In this way, squabbling over a favored spot will be greatly reduced. Once the birds have paired off and selected a box, the spares can be removed. It should also be remembered that in aviary situations, any unpaired birds should also be removed as they might become a nuisance to the others once breeding is underway.

In order to encourage the birds to commence nest building, it is best to place some soft hay or dry grass in the nest, maybe even a few feathers. Ensure that there is a plentiful supply of suitable materials on hand for the birds to use. Once nests have been built, remove all potential material. Otherwise the cock, in particular, may continue to add to the nest after the hen has laid.

If the birds show no interest in the nest box, either they are not quite in full breeding condition or they just do not like your choice of box—or maybe its position. Watch the hen, especially in pens or aviaries, and she may indicate where she prefers to have her eggs by trying to start building at another point. Some actually prefer to be very low to the ground, even on it. If this is her choice then place the box in such

may take a little longer than this. Such seeds contain increased protein and vitamin content and are much liked by Zebra Finches—millet and canary seed are choice seeds but any will germinate. Failure to germinate by about 36 hours means the seed is of poor quality, so a fresh supplier might be the order of the day. Germinating trays can be purchased but are not essential as any suitable receptacle will suffice.

attack the youngsters if they persist (which they usually do) in entering the nest box. In aviary situations, this is less of a problem, but most breeders nonetheless still separate the young Zebras once they can look after themselves.

If you live in the more temperate parts of the world, or the colder, wetter areas, then young Zebras are best placed indoors if the weather is changeable. A sudden downpour

A finch egg is a tiny thing, indeed. This is a hatched egg and some wood shavings.

After the chicks are fledged, they will return each night to their nest, but about a week after fledging, they should be weaned and independent of their parents. In cages, it is best if they are removed once they are self-feeding as the hen will want to get on with the business of laying a second round of eggs. She may even

of rain can soak youngsters whose feathers absorb water quickly; in such a state they are unable to fly and may go unnoticed on the aviary floor, under a bush, or elsewhere and may quickly succumb to chilling.

FOSTERING
One advantage of having

This 11-day-old Zebra Finch chick is developing nicely. You can see some feather development and tufts of down on its head and back.

numerous pairs breeding at the same time is that if for any reason a hen dies, or takes no interest in her chicks, it is possible to foster them to another pair. The important consideration is that they are placed only with pairs whose own eggs or chicks are at the same state of development. Otherwise, their chances of survival are reduced greatly because they will be unable to compete with more advanced chicks for food. Bengalese are also excellent foster parents, but if fostered under another species, the Zebras are imprinted with that species and may be unwilling to mate with their own kind in later life.

Hybridization with other species is quite common with Zebra Finches, and the following are just a few of the other finches with whom Zebras have produced chicks: Bicheno, Star, Bengalese, Diamond Firetail, Tricolored Nun, Masked, Bloack-throated, African Silverbill, Java Sparrow, Indian Silverbill, and the Plum-headed Finch.

Were they ever to hybridize with finches carrying colors such as blue or green—and if these proved fertile and were established—the possibilities opened up would dramatically boost the already great interest in color breeding.

RINGING

When the chicks are about a week old, they can have closed rings placed on them. This is a simple procedure in which the three longer toes are placed through the ring, which is slid up the lower shank and over the fourth, shorter rear toe. It is best if you watch an experienced breeder do this first after which you will feel confident. It does not hurt the chick. The chick should be held upside down, firmly yet gently, though it may squeak as much because it is being handled than because of any discomfort.

Apart from closed metal rings, you can purchase split metal or plastic colored rings, which can serve as temporary identification of chicks from differing pairs.

When any form of ring is placed on a chick, it must be checked periodically to ensure it is not clogged with feces or any other material, which could create blood flow problems.

BREEDING FREQUENCY

A pair of Zebras should not be expected to rear more than three good rounds of chicks in any one season. That they are capable of doing so is beyond question and up to 19 successive broods have been reared! Any breeders who expect more than four clutches per year are, frankly, greedy. Their birds are indeed unfortunate in having such owners. Nor should young birds be expected to rear strong clutches. While Zebras as young as eight weeks old are capable of breeding, I would suggest that nine months is soon enough, as such birds will be really mature and capable of producing vigorous youngsters.

RECORD BOOKS

From the moment you commence breeding, it is beneficial to keep detailed records of all that goes on in your aviaries as this will be very useful in helping to avoid—or track down—later problems. The records should tell you how many eggs a given pair produced, how many hatched and how many were reared. Of those eggs that did not hatch records should show how many were clear and how many were dead-in-shell. The dates of matings, incubation period, fledging times, and notes indicating any special diets supplied should all appear in your records. Even apparently insignificant happenings are worthy of noting as they may well, at some future date, have meaning to you. A growing number of bird keepers are now committing their records to home computers. From computers you can call up all kinds of information at the touch of a key.

BREEDING PROBLEMS

One of the most common problems within all forms of domesticated species is progressive lack of fertility within a population. An obvious cause of this is the degree of inbreeding within both a single breeder's strain and within the population as a whole. Only by checking your records can you tell if the incidence of infertility is increasing. If so, then the answer is to carefully introduce fresh genes from another breeder's strain—but only after conducting a series of matings to check that the lines are compatible and producing the desired effect.

Another potential cause of infertility is the habitual breeding of very young birds. Initially, things may seem fine, but the strain may tell a year or two later. Yet another factor which is often overlooked, is related to the very fact that in captivity many birds are reared that in the wild would have perished. For example, hens will sometimes fail to incubate eggs or ignore chicks. This may be directly attributable to an obvious problem, i.e., diet, stress, and so on, but in other cases it is as though the hen knows something is not right so ignores the egg. By intervening and placing eggs or

An 8-day-old chick opens wide in anticipation of being fed by its parents.

chicks under foster parents, we are able to rear such chicks. Now, they may well appear to be fine Zebras as they grow, but they may not be so fine could we but closely examine their reproductive organs or genetic makeup. Such birds, with a predisposition to infertility, may then be used for breeding, and so, on the problem goes—increasing in incidence with successive generations until it reaches doomsday point—total infertility.

In the wild, only the fit survive to breed, so vigor is maintained in the species. We are able to interrupt natural selection and not always to the benefit of the species. Here again, records are the key, and this is where compromise comes in because we select for good looks more than for vigor. The answer is that we should breed only from the best birds, including breeding and rearing performance, even if that means overlooking a few exceptionally beautiful-looking individuals—not an easy decision to make.

Eggbinding

This problem can be genetic, or it can be the direct result of incorrect diet or lack of exercise. The eggshell is too soft and cannot be moved along the oviduct because it "gives" when the hen contracts her muscles. Alternatively, due to overweight, the muscles themselves may not be able to push the egg on its outward journey. Either way, the hen should immediately be placed into a hospital cage, when heat alone will hopefully bring forth the egg. Should it not, then it must be removed surgically by your vet—if he can get to you before the hen dies. Such a hen should not be returned for breeding until she is fully fit. Any eggs she has already laid should be fostered or destroyed, as the chances are they will be less than ideal anyway.

Hen Fails to Feed Young

Beyond the fact that a hen may just be a bad mother, you should check whether there are signs of mites in the nest box, for infestations will certainly put a hen off feeding her chicks—and they may well kill the chicks as well. A stressed hen will also fail to rear her chicks, in which case you must ponder if anything has suddenly changed in her environment that may have upset her. An overly attentive cock can put a hen off laying or incubating and his removal for a couple of days should effect a cure. Once she has settled to the job at hand, he will usually be put in his place when he is returned to her.

Dead-in-shell

This can be caused by infection getting into a scratched egg—the scratch may not be visible to the eye. Another cause of this can be lack of humidity in the nest box—more frequently met when birds are bred indoors in cages. Light spraying of the box during very warm weather will be helpful. Double-shelled eggs may prevent the chick from cutting its way out, in which case it has, in effect, drowned in the liquid within the egg. All cases of dead-in-shell should be recorded in order that you can see if the problem has any genetic base.

Sometimes the hen will not feed her young. Not this one! She has brought grass into the nest for her chicks.

Feather Plucking

Sometimes a hen will pluck the feathers from young chicks. Such birds tend to become habitual pluckers thereafter. They should not be used for future breeding, and a careful watch should be made on her chicks to see if the trait is passed to them. Likewise, hens may become eggeaters. This is rare, however, but again, such birds have no place in your breeding room.

Only those breeders who apply the most rigorous standards to their breeding stock will ultimately succeed in producing reliable breeding lines—along the way many otherwise fine birds will be discarded.

COLOR VARIETIES

The descriptions detailed in this chapter are basic because the numerous illustrations found throughout this book will give a very clear picture of the various colors found in Zebra Finches. The reader is then advised to see as many examples as possible before deciding which colors he favors for breeding. (The size of the species is 10.75-11.5 cm [4.25-4.5 in]).

WILD OR NORMAL GRAY
Cock—The head is gray as is the neck, which is then merged into a brown on the back and wings. The beak is red-orange and is bordered by a fine line of black feathers that extend down from the middle line of the top mandible to the lower beak. The feathers between the beak and cheek patches form a line below the eye and extend down just below the lower beak. They are white and bordered at the cheeks by black feathers. The cheek patches are a rich chestnut-brown. The throat and upper chest is barred with black feathers on a white ground color, this ending with a solid band of black from flank to flank across the chest—the minimum requirement of this black bar is 3.2 mm ($^1/_8$ in). The lower chest and abdomen is white, becoming tinged with tan at the thighs and vent. The tail feathers are white barred with black. The legs are orange and the eyes are black with a red-brown iris. The flanks are chestnut-brown well spotted with white dots.

Hen—Lacks the cheek patches, chest barring, and flank color and spots. The beak is usually a paler shade of color. The areas barred in cocks are replaced by a light gray in the hen, as are the cheek patches and flanks.

DOMINANT SILVER
The silver mutation appears like a dilution of the normal gray, and the cheek patches may range from pale orange to cream. The hen, likewise, is a paler version of the normal hen.

An example of a dominant silver Zebra Finch, whose coloring appears like a dilution of the normal grey.

This mutation first appeared in Australia prior to World War II and reached Europe during the same period, but nothing is known about its origin. When a second silver mutation appeared in Denmark, the two were treated as one for some time until it was realized that they were in fact separate mutations, the newer one being a recessive while the Australian mutation was dominant to the normal wild gray type. The dominant silver is not as popular today as in past years. The eminent Zebra Finch authority Cyril Rogers believes this to be due to its being used to improve dilute fawns. Careful linebreeding is needed to retain good silvers free from a tendency to show fawn in their plumage.

DOMINANT CREAM

This is a dilute fawn. Here the gray is replaced by a soft cream on the head, but the intensity of the cream can vary between light and dark. The cheek patches are edged with gray rather than black, and the chest barring is likewise a gray color. The hen has the same color as the cock, less the usual markings.

This mutation also originated in Australia and may even have been the precursor of the dominant silver.

WHITE

The plumage should be as white as possible, the hens often being slightly paler. You will see faint traces of gray or fawn markings in some specimens. The beak, legs,

A beautiful white Zebra Finch who with its black eyes cannot be mistaken for an albino.

This little bird is a Pied Gray, and his normal colors appear in patches on his body.

and eyes are colored as for normals, so you should not confuse a white with an albino (in which the eyes are red).

This mutation dates back to at least 1921, when it first became known from a strain bred in Sydney. When breeding whites, it is essential that selection be rigid in order to reduce the incidence of fawn or gray markings. Outcrosses, when required, should be to fawns or normal grays.

PIED GRAY

In this mutation, the gray or any other coloring of the normal gray bird is broken so as to appear in patches. The missing color is replaced by white, and ideally 50% of the color should appear white, but this not to include the white of the underparts. It is preferred that the broken areas are balanced, but this is very difficult to achieve. The hen lacks the usual markings of hens but otherwise should be marked as the cock.

Pieds were first recorded in Denmark about 1935 and proved very popular, quickly becoming established in all European countries. They are not quite as popular in Australia. The pied is available in all forms, but the grays and fawns are undoubtably the most popular, as the mutation is the most striking in these forms. Fawns are the same as grays, but the gray areas are replaced by fawn.

Although breeding pieds is no problem, the difficulty is obtaining well-matched pairs for exhibition purposes because pieds are so variable in their markings. The genetic state of pieds is very complex. Although they are normal recessives (though the fawn is sex-linked), the factors controlling the actual break-up of color is not well understood and is certainly not predictable for how the areas of white will be placed.

PENGUIN

In the penguin mutation of the normal gray, the colors are all diluted; the feathers of the back and wings are edged with lighter gray to give a lace-like effect. The chest barring is totally absent. Birds of this mutation are seen at their best after their second molt. The hens are as the cocks, but the cheek patches are white. This mutation was known in Australia during the 1940s and was believed to have been introduced to Europe in 1950 or thereabouts. The original birds of this color were somewhat smaller than other zebras, and this restricted their popularity because good-type birds were difficult to produce, the color being linked to the smaller size. While specialty fanciers have improved type in penguins, the mutation, nonetheless, is not one followed with the same enthusiasm as are other varieties—no doubt reflecting the difficulty in producing good exhibition-quality birds. Penguins can be had in the other mutations, but the gray and fawn, being more striking, are the more popular.

RECESSIVE SILVER

This color variety is similar to the dominant silver already described, but a good recessive is a somewhat more even shade of silver than the dominant, though possibly slightly darker. This, however, is a relative statement because much depends on the depth of gray in the normals from which they were developed. Being a recessive, they lost popularity against the dominant silver and are not popular today in the UK, the USA or Australia—though they maintain a select and dedicated band of followers. There are many recessive silvers spread within normal grays, as is evident from their appearance in what breeders thought were pure grays—the sudden arrival of silver chicks from such matings clearly establishes the fact that both parents were, in fact, gray/silver.

The recessive cream is similar to its dominant counterpart but is slightly darker. Again, it does not enjoy quite the popularity it deserves but, like the silver, has suffered in the availability of a more easily bred variety, the dominant cream.

FAWN

The fawn is colored as the normal except that the head and back, together with the wings, are a fawn color. The throat barring is of a brownish black. Hen as for normal gray hen but the gray replaced by fawn as in the fawn cock.

This mutation goes back to the 1920s, when fawns were seen in a wild flock, and a pair were eventually caught and sent to Adelaide where they were bred.

The Penguin mutation, shown here, is differentiated by light gray edges along the back and wing feathers and a more dilute shading overall.

Originally, there were two forms recognized, the cinnamon and the fawn, but it was then realized they were merely variations of the same mutation and fawn became accepted as the correct description.

While fawns are used to improve color in other varieties, the fawns themselves are best bred continually to fawns, but with careful selection made to match the evenness of both of the proposed pair. If an outcross is needed it is best achieved with a normal gray—the usual need being to improve a type feature. However, should a suitable-quality bird not be available, then another colored bird can be used.

When selecting pairs, be careful that a good bird is not discarded because of apparent unevenness of color that has been created by lost feathers being renewed and appearing darker than those which have faded—this, of course, applies to all varieties where light feathers are concerned.

CHESTNUT-FLANKED WHITE

This is a very attractive mutation in which white replaces the gray on the head, back, and wings. The cheek patches are orange rather than chestnut, and it is preferred that the chest barrings are missing, but the black band on the chest is retained. In most examples,

The Fawn is colored normally except that his back and wing feathers are fawn rather than gray, and his chest is a brownish-black barring. This is a Crested Fawn.

The Chestnut-Flanked White is a striking mutation first seen in wild flocks in Australia around 1936.

however, faint barring of chest and throat will be seen. The hen is the same as the cock, but the cheek patches are white.

This mutation, often abbreviated to CFW, was also first seen in wild flocks, about 1936, in Queensland. Examples were caught and were known in Australia as marked whites and were quickly established before finding their way to Europe and to the USA. Surprisingly, they lost favor in their homelands, but more are seen these days. CFW can be had in the other varieties but is seen at its best in grays and fawns.

Unless great attention is paid to pairings, then CFWs will develop an off-white, almost cream, coloration, so efforts should be made to breed only with good white examples. Normal gray is the most favored outcross should type or good strong cheek patch colors need "freshening up."

ALBINO

A good albino must be pure white throughout its plumage, with no faint barring or other marks evident as are often seen in whites. The iris is red, and the beak is red-orange with the legs orange. The beak of the hen may be a slightly paler red, but otherwise the sexes are very similar.

Albinos are thought to have made their first appearance in the 1950s in Australia, but they may well have been in evidence at a much earlier date and been regarded as whites. Albinos arrived in Europe and elsewhere but did not gain the support that they have in Australia and are still comparative rarities.

BLACK-BREASTED

This is similar to the normal gray, but the black band of the chest extends well up to just below the throat. Thus, there is no barring. The flank white spots are more elongated than round. The tail feathers are brown with black marks on them, and the black tear markings that edge the cheek patches are much reduced or absent. This mutation, which is an autosomal recessive, is gaining in popularity. The split birds of this mutation can be detected from normals because the cheek patches are larger and the breast bar is wider, indicating that the normal dominant form does not exhibit full dominance in this particular case.

LIGHT-BACKS

These birds are normal gray birds but their head, back, and wings are silver. The mutation is believed to have first appeared in Switzerland and is being established in the UK by Cyril Rogers. Once firmly established, this should prove a quite popular variety, as the black markings of the normal gray contrast nicely with the dilution of gray on the other parts.

SADDLE- BACK

In this variety, a patch or saddle of gray or fawn is seen on the shoulder and base of the neck in white birds. This is considered to be merely heavy flecking, but Cyril Rogers postulates that it could be a new mutation that has appeared but is eclipsed by flecked whites. He points out that only a series of test matings will resolve which it is. However, if it is not a separate mutation, then it could still become established as a variety if selective breeding was conducted with heavily marked whites showing this saddle appearance.

GRIZZLE

In this variety, the normal gray areas of the bird are mottled with white specks. It is Australian in origin and still rather rare outside of that country, where it is believed to be an autosomal recessive in mode of transmission.

CRESTED

This mutation is not a color but refers to the tuft of feathers on the head. These feathers may form a complete or partially complete rosette, and the crest mutation can be found in all colors. The origin of the mutation is not known, but it was first reported by Herman Heinzel, who acquired

Two pairs of Light-Backs perch on a twig, showing off their silvery heads.

specimens in Spain. Cyril Rogers received a cock crested bird from Heinzel and was probably one of the first breeders of this form in the UK.

YELLOW BEAK

For some years this mutation was ignored, as it was considered to be purely a poorly colored normal. However, specimens were unintentionally bred and slowly came the recognition that it was indeed a mutation. It is now a recognized variety, and yellow beaks can be shown alongside the normal red beaks. They have a growing specialty following that is attempting to improve the quality of the color, which can range from a yellow to orange-yellow.

BLACK

There have been various claims over the years that a black mutation had been found, but none of the claims were ever substantiated. It is probable that in all cases, the birds in question were suffering from a nutritional deficiency or had an abnormality that affected the plumage but was not of genetic origin. However, it is most likely that one day a black mutation will appear and should create quite a stir when it does.

HEALTH MATTERS

The potential number of diseases that a Zebra Finch can suffer or die from is legion. However, in nearly all cases, the reason can be traced back to poor management. For this reason, providing the breeder applies common sense and good hygiene to stock management, then trouble will largely be avoided, or be of a minor nature, which is acceptable, though not desired, in any aviary or birdroom situation.

The possible causes of ailments are numerous, so the first objective is to keep them to a minimum. The first thing that must be done is to ensure that freshly acquired birds are always subjected to a three-week period of isolation, away from your other stock. This gives you the time to check that they are not already incubating some disease.

Next, we should consider which birds are at most risk and from what. Young birds can easily become chilled so they are at risk in outside aviaries during the early spring and late autumn. In a chilled state, a bird will quickly succumb to the most minor of other ailments that it would normally overcome with no problem. The answer is to bring in your stock if the weather looks at all changeable.

Aviary birds are at risk from the droppings of wild birds, which can introduce a host of bacteria. Aviary floors should be cleaned at least once per week, more often if possible. Perches in the flight should be periodically replaced and certainly cleaned on a regular basis to remove possible wild-bird droppings. This applies to all perchs, as dirty ones no doubt account for most of the foot sores seen in birds. Those caged for long periods are especially susceptible due to sand or grit (the cage-floor lining) that clings to their feet when they are perching.

Overcrowded birds are at obvious risk both on account of the stress such a situation creates and because an illness in just one bird will quickly be passed to others in the same cage or aviary. Birdrooms are a very-high risk area because the number of birds is invariably quite high. Only by maintaining scrupulous hygiene can we keep the risk down to an acceptable level. Your hands should be washed before handling birds and likewise after each one has been handled.

Most breeders store their seed and other foods in their birdrooms, but it is actually better if all foods can be stored and prepared in an alternative place. Bacteria from an ailing bird can quickly contaminate the seed, foods, and similar items. However, often this is not possible, so the next best thing is to at least cover all food items and, if possible, have a small room for food preparation in the birdroom.

The casual transferring of birds from one cage to another is not to be recommended unless you are really sure that your overall standard of hygiene is as good as it could be—be honest now, is it? If you are willing to admit that you are lax in this or that, then there is every hope that at least you appreciate the importance of hygiene beyond paying it lip service.

CHILLS

All birds are at risk from chilling, and any that are subjected to drafts are especially so. At the first sign of a bird sitting with its feathers all fluffed, and maybe a nasal or eye discharge, then capture it and place it in a stock cage with an infra-red lamp, maintaining a steady 29°C (85°F). A temperature much below this may be too low. Heat alone is probably the nearest thing you will find to a "cure-all" remedy. The addition of syrup of buckthorn to the water is an age-old treatment as is the addition of glycerine and honey to water, or a drop of whisky.

Once a bird has received heat treatment, it must be gradually acclimatized back to its normal aviary or cage temperature; otherwise, it will most likely become ill again. During heat treatment, the bird should be able to move into or away from the source of heat as it feels most comfortable. If it cannot, it will quickly stress, thus defeating the whole object. I would withdraw greenfood at such times. When a bird is recovering from an illness, it will generally appreciate some softfood—either one of the commercial brands or bread and milk to which honey or sugar has been added. Pour hot water or milk over the bread and press out the excess to create a moist pulp. Should the patient show no interest, then some spray millet scattered over the softfood will usually do the trick—or any other favored tidbit.

DIARRHEA

If your birds show unduly copious feces, this may be a minor problem, or it could be symptomatic of much worse to come. Immediate isolation and heat treatment is needed. Should the bird not improve within 24 hours, call your veterinarian, and ideally have available a fecal specimen that can be taken for microscopy. All greenfood should be withheld. It sometimes happens that in the spring, the sudden availability of much greenfood prompts the birds to glut on it, so give greenfood on a gradual basis once supplies are plentiful.

MITES

There are numerous species of mite that can affect birds. Some live away from the host while others live on it. All mites are small arthropods. Possibly the most difficult to eradicate is the red mite *Dermanyssus gallinae*. This is a very obnoxious creepy-crawly that leaves its hiding places at night to venture forth and suck the blood of the birds before returning to its place of refuge. It is visible to the eye as a grayish red, quick-moving pest. It is common in wild birds and poultry so could easily become established if you were less than diligent about cleaning perches and the crevices of cages. Severe infestations can debilitate a bird to the point of anemia. Such birds will quickly succumb to secondary infection in their weakened state.

The remedy is one of the numerous acaricides that can be sprayed over the cages. Ideally, repaint the cages—even if on a rotational basis over a month or two. This should solve the problem. Nest boxes must be carefully checked, while perches are best burned and replaced. By treating for red mite, you will automatically eradicate any other members of this group of external pests. It has to be said that infestation levels are the result of a poor cleaning routine.

DAMAGED LIMBS

Small cuts will be no problem and will need only careful swabbing with a mild disinfectant, but broken limbs are more difficult to treat. Small splints from a matchstick can be secured in place with cotton, but beware of having the splint too tight. A broken leg will take about 14 days to knot together again, after which the bird should be fine, though it may thereafter not hold its leg in its previous position. Broken wings need to be carefully placed back into position, after which little more can be done. The bird in both cases should be placed in isolation in a comfortable temperature and disturbed as little as possible. If in doubt, consult your veterinarian.

Your Zebra Finch will stay perky and chipper with regular maintenance of his cage, including washing all eating and drinking receptacles.

Baths are an important part of overall good finch health. The clean water helps slough off dirt and bacteria that settle on feathers.

GENERAL CONSIDERATIONS

What is most important to appreciate where finches and other small birds are concerned is that an ill bird one hour can be dead the next, such is the speed of their metabolism. For this reason, daily inspection of all stock is essential and *any* that do not look their usual perky selves must be quickly given heat treatment, as tomorrow may be too late.

It is not usually feasible to inject finches because the shock will kill them, and many antibiotics cannot be administered via drinking the water, as this is an unreliable method of dosing any bird. Often, the exact nature of an illness cannot be established until after the patient has died because so many avian illnesses and diseases exhibit the same clinical signs. This being so, it is always worthwhile to have your vet arrange a post-mortem—especially if there seems no reason for the illness. For the cost involved you may get an early warning that could prevent a serious problem in your birdroom.

EXHIBITION

There is little doubt that once a breeder has established a growing number of birds in an aviary or birdroom, the desire to exhibit becomes progressively stronger. The only way it is possible to tell just how good your stock is will be by directly comparing it with that of others in a competitive situation. However, there is much more to showing than just the actual competition, for it is a social world in itself. At a bird show, you will meet new friends and be able to discuss the merits, or otherwise, of many birds. You will meet breeders of other species. Ideas and problems can be exchanged on a whole range of matters, from feeding to aviaries to ailments.

At the bigger shows, there will be specialty booths selling everything needed by breeders, so that, all in all, it is a fascinating aspect of bird keeping.

The would-be competitor is strongly advised to visit a number of shows before actually entering birds. In this way you can see the way birds are "staged," the general way things are organized, and get the feel of the whole atmosphere. There are many types of shows, which will vary not only from country to country but from the type of show itself. There are small local events that are very informal and usually supported only by those in the immediate area of the show—these are ideal events in which to gain experience and are often limited to members of the club staging the show. Larger events, which any person can enter, are called open shows, and they vary considerably in size based on the number of classes they schedule. Each society that plans an exhibition will estimate how many entries it is likely to receive and determine the number of classes based on this. Zebra finches are always well represented as they have a very large following at shows. The biggest shows will attract thousands of entries and may be staged over two or even three days. National societies for Zebra Finches will also hold their own shows and wins at these events are especially coveted.

A pair of Chestnut Flanked White Zebra Finches are shown here in a show cage for judges and fellow exhibitors to admire.